A tricky

Fun with all sorts of puzzley things

Patrick Forsyth and Trevor Peters

This book contains material the original source of
which is impossible to trace with any certainty. Some
exists in many variants and could come from
everything from traditional material from long ago to
that recycled on Christmas crackers. Apologies to
anyone who might feel an acknowledgement may be
necessary; please advise and that could be included
in any reprint.

This edition Published by Touchstonetc (Maldon).
 ISBN: 9798864871218
The authors may be contacted via
www.patrickforsyth.com

Introduction

This book contains a number of "puzzles" each posing a problem which needs a bit of thought to work out. They are all selected to be a little bit tricky, many involve words or numbers and sometimes both and those included have been chosen to create a real mixture in both type of problem and complexity.

Take note: some problems may appear more difficult than they are, for example one may seem to need complicated mathematics, but may not need maths at all. There is sometimes a trick or shortcut that makes the solution easy to find once you have discovered the trick. Look out for clues that may be hidden in the way a problem is described. Some have a lesson within them, a moral that is worth taking note of as it presents a useful thought.

All are presented so that it is necessary to turn over a page to find the solution, so you can avoid the answer pages if you want to give yourself longer to think about something in order to find a solution. You can choose to do some against the clock, and once you have the answer you can try them out on friends and family. Alternatively, some might be done alongside others as a race to see who finishes first.

Along the way the puzzles are punctuated with some fun facts, some fantastic, some weird, and some riddles, some just silly, some needing a little thought. The answer to the riddles is printed upside down at the bottom of the page – so you may not want to look until you have given them a moment's thought. So, puzzle away... and have fun!

As you start, remember the old saying:
'If you think you can, you can and if you think you can't, you're right!'

Fun with your name

Now let's start with something that is surely easy. You just need to know your own name and have a pencil and a sheet of paper.

The task: Draw a horizontal line two or three inches across and write the first and last letters of your first name at each end of the line.

You can do it here if you want (but only if it is your own book!).

Done that? Okay - now turn over and see if you did it correctly.

What is as light as a feather, yet can only be held for a short time?

Answer:

Remember, you were asked to use your own name. We may all have different names, of course, so let's show an example and use the names Sean or Susan. The instruction was to: Draw a horizontal line two or three inches long and write the first and last letters of your first name at each end of the line. Okay? Write the first and last letters of either of these names at either end of the line and what you get is ***not***:

S_____N

Rather it must be: **SN_____SN**

How so? ... because the instruction clearly said: write the first *and* last letter of your first name at *each* end of the line.

The first version, with only a single letter at each end of the line, may somehow seem logical initially but the moral here is that with any problem the first thing to do is to be *absolutely sure* that you understand the question completely accurately... and here it clearly referred to writing *the first and last letters* of your name. So well done if you got this right first time.

Fun fact: fantastic or weird?

The tallest tower ever built out of Lego bricks was made in Italy.

It stood just over 35 metres tall and used more than 550,000 bricks.

A record just waiting to be broken and which could be surpassed at any moment!

Joining the crosses

Below is an arrangement of nine crosses, set out so that they are the same distance apart in every direction.

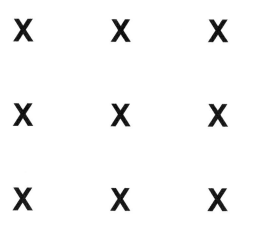

The task is to draw a line which goes through every cross, using only four straight lines and without taking your pen or pencil off the paper as you do so.

Draw this out on paper and have a go.

Answer:

How you do this is shown below. We tend to see the arrangement as a shape – a square, and then somehow we feel we should find a solution within that square shape.

The lines can only be drawn by drawing outside of the "square" arrangement as in the arrangement below.

Fun fact: fantastic or weird?

Are you sitting comfortably? And are you sitting *still*? You may well be comfortable, but you are not still. Why? Because we are all always moving. The fact that the Earth rotates on its axis and also orbits the Sun and that the whole solar system orbits the Milky Way galaxy provides a complicated calculation, but the end result is that, even when you are sitting still, you are moving at about 500,000 mile per hour.

What is stronger than steel but cannot handle the sun?

Answer

ɘɔI

A little bit odd

Read this next paragraph carefully and see if you can answer the question it poses

As you scan this short paragraph, try to spot what is unusual about it. Half an hour is normal for many to find a solution that is both logical and satisfactory to its originator. I do not say that anything is "wrong" about it, simply that it is unusual. You may want to study its grammatical construction to find out why it is so odd, but that is not a basis of its abnormality, nor is its lack of any information, logical points or conclusion. If you think about words, you may find that an aid to solving this particular conundrum as it is unusual. So, why is that?

Do you want a little clue? If so, then examine the question about a clue just posed above, in bold type - this is *not* written to be odd in the same way as the paragraph posing the problem. Does that help? If not, then you will find the answer over the page.

What has a head
and a tail,
but no body?

Answer:

The letter that occurs most often in normal writing is the letter "e" More than 10% of the letters in any average text consist of letter Es. It is really pretty difficult to write very many words at all without using that letter – but the paragraph posing the question here does not contain a single letter "e" – that makes it read and sound a little awkward and it is therefore somewhat odd because of that. Easy now.

Fun fact: fantastic or weird?

If you start with a single penny and were able to double it every day for just a single month, then after 30 days you would have more than five *million* pounds (actually you would have exactly £5,368,709.12p).

Crossing the river

Consider the following problem: a man is travelling with a fox, a chicken and a bag of grain. He proceeds with care as the fox wants to eat the chicken and the chicken wants to eat the grain.

He comes to and must cross a river, and finds a tiny boat moored at the bank that should help, but it is so small that it will only carry himself and one other thing. If he leaves the fox and the chicken together, he will have no chicken (it will get eaten); similarly, he can't leave the chicken with the grain.

Given that only one can be transported at a time, how does he get all three to the other side without mishap?

How do you make the number one disappear?

Answer

Just add the letter G in front of it – and it's gone!

Answer:

Making the river crossing successfully needs a bit of juggling. Let's list the stages:

1. First, he takes the chicken across, leaving it there as he returns.
2. Then he takes the bag of grain across, leaves it ashore and brings the chicken back with him.
3. Next, he takes the fox across leaving the chicken on the original side of the river.
4. Last, with the fox and the grain safe on the far side he returns again and collects the chicken.

He then has all three safely across the water and can – carefully – continue his journey.

Fun fact: fantastic or weird?

Do you ever tell someone you will be 'there in a jiffy'? Be careful: because a jiffy actually means $1/100^{th}$ of a second – and it is a fair bet that's not what you are saying.

Word transformation

Add each of the two-word combinations below together to get a whole new word.

Example: to shout + what you say when you feel pain = a colour. The answer here is the word yellow (yell + ow).

1. A light brown colour + to leave = a dance.
2. A store's announcement + a type of women's clothing = a building's location.
3. A vehicle + an animal pal = a floor covering.
4. The ocean + a father's boy = part of the year.
5. Another name for dad + a yellow veggie = a white fluffy snack.

Turn over the page for the answers.

What word becomes shorter when you add two additional letters to it?

The word Short (add the letters e and r to the end).

Answer:

The words here are as follows:

1. tan + go = tango.
2. ad + dress = address.
3. car + pet = carpet
4. sea + son = season.
5. pop + corn = popcorn.

Fun fact: fantastic or weird?

Every odd number when written as words contains a letter e.

Logical arrangement of countries

There is a logic to the sequence in which the countries here are listed:

1. **Cyprus**
2. **Sweden**
3. **Morocco**

The question is: which country logically comes next in this sequence and why?

Answer:

If you look at the list of countries, you will see that the number of identical vowels they contain increases as you go down the list: one U in Cyprus, two Es in Sweden, three Os in Morocco – so the next one would be a country containing four examples of the same vowel: it is **Madagascar.**

You will find that the only country which contains all the vowels is **Mosambique.**

People on a train

Now some numbers: There is a number of people travelling on a train It stops at a station and 19 additional people get on. The train continues along the line and when it stops at the next station 17 people get off.

At this point there are 63 people on board. The question is how many people were on the train to begin with?

Answer:

If 19 new passengers got on the train at the first stop and 17 disembarked at the next, then by simple subtraction, 19 – 17 = 2, having started with 63, there are 2 more at the end. The answer must be **65**.

What can you hold
in your right hand
but not in your left?

Answer

Your left hand

Fun fact: fantastic or weird?

The Romans had no symbol for 0 (zero).
No wonder Roman numerals are complicated.

Finding the fruit

There are three wooden crates, one containing apples, one with oranges, and one with a mixture of both apples and oranges. Each crate is closed and labelled with one of three labels: Apples, Oranges, or Apples and Oranges. If you know the labelling is *incorrect*, how could you pick just one fruit from one crate to figure out what is really in each crate?

Answer:

Pick a piece of fruit from the crate marked Apples and Oranges. If that fruit is an apple, you know that the crate should be labelled Apples because you know all of the labels are incorrect as they are and thus it cannot hold what it says. Therefore, you then know that the crate marked Apples must be Oranges (if it were labelled Apples and Oranges, the Oranges crate would be labelled correctly, and we know it isn't), and the one marked Oranges is Apples and Oranges. Alternately, if you picked an orange from the crate marked Apples and Oranges, you know that crate should be marked Oranges, the one marked Oranges must be Apples, and the one marked Apples must be Apples and Oranges.

Topsy turvey numbers

Here the task is to work out which number logically fills the blank in the following sequence:

16   06   68   88   __   98

This may be a bit tricky, indeed you may decide that your mathematical ability is not up to it - but don't worry, that ability doesn't matter!

What is it that can be made to disappear with just a single word?

Answer

Silence

Answer:

As the clue suggested this needs no mathematical ability at all, well, other than your being able to count.

If you turn the page upside down, you will see it then shows a new sequence of numbers that reads:

86 __ 88 89 90 91

So, to logically fill the gap all you need to do is count! And the answer is thus **87.**

Turn me on my side I am everything. Cut me in half and I am nothing. What am I?

Random or ordered?

What explains why this seemingly odd sequence of number is in the order it is: **854,917,632**?

𝓕𝓾𝓷 𝓯𝓪𝓬𝓽: fantastic or weird?

Compared with our Sun the Earth is tiny. In fact, the Sun contains 99.86% of all the matter in the Solar System; and it would take 1.3 million Earth-sized bodies to fill the Sun.

Answer:

The numbers **854,917,632** are arranged in alphabetical order by the first letter of the words: eight, five... and so on.

What four-letter word can be written forward, backwards – and upside down?

Rare spelling

Apart from some proper names, like Woorree Park (which is a place in Western Australia), very few words contain three separate incidences of double letters.

Without using proper names, can you think of one (or two – there are two that are words which are closely associated) that have this unusual feature?

Answer:

One such word is **Bookkeeper** and a second, closely related, is **Bookkeeping**. And, apart from proper names, the authors thought for a long, long time, but could think of no others. If you can, do let us know!

Very orderly numbers

This involves thinking about counting.
Imagine counting sequentially through the numbers – 1, 2, 3, 4 and so on, but writing the numbers out in words: one, two, three higher and higher.

Imagine also that you must then arrange the written numbers into alphabetical order (so, for instance forty-two would come earlier that sixty-seven).

The question is when will you come to the first **odd** number? Will that number be in the:

1. **Hundreds**
2. **Thousands**
3. **Millions**
4. *Even* **higher?**

This just needs thinking about; writing it out might take far too long.
Just how big do you think the number would be?

Answer:

First, you should have worked out that eight, beginning with an e, is the lowest number in terms of the alphabet. So, *all* the many numbers starting with eight must lead the way when every number is written in an A – Z order.

Is the first odd number to be listed in the hundreds? No. Nor is it in the thousands or millions – it is very much higher. The first odd number will be: **8,000,000,085.**

Makes you say Wow! Doesn't it? And now you know why the instructions to this puzzle suggested you did not actually write a list!

Number to words

Use nine matchsticks to spell out the number 100 (the noughts will be square shaped, but the number will be clear).

Now the task is to change this by moving only *two* matches to make not another number, but rather a word – the word CAT.

Have a go, if you get stuck then you will find the answer is over the page.

What can you
make, but never
touch or see it?

You make a noise

Answer:

Here the way the two matchsticks need to be moved is shown below, then it is only necessary to turn the page and look at it sideways to see the word CAT!

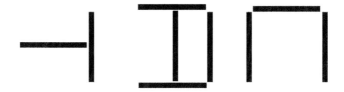

Move the bottom matchstick of the second (righthand) zero and place it vertically halfway across the first (lefthand) zero and move the lefthand vertical stick from the left hand zero placing it horizontally to the left of the figure one.

𝓕𝓾𝓷 𝓯𝓪𝓬𝓽: fantastic or weird?

There are ten times more stars in the universe than there are grains of sand on the entire Earth, yet on a dark night you can only see about 3000 stars in a clear night sky (though a different 3000 is visible if you are in the Southern hemisphere).

Fewer Squares

Arrange some matchsticks as in the way illustrated below.

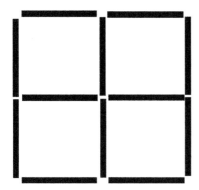

Now, by removing only *two* of the matchsticks turn the arrangement into one of just two squares only.

What two kinds of
building has the
most stories?

Answer:

The arrangement shown below gives you two squares.

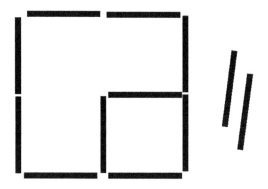

Where do you find tomorrow coming before yesterday?

In a dictionary

Where on the list?

Consider this list of numbers:

1 2 6 __
4 5 9 __
3 7 8 __

There is a logic to the order of each line. The task is to add the number 10 to one of the lines, but where does it logically fit? The answer needs to include the reason why. Can you work it out?

Fun fact: fantastic or weird?

'Schoolmaster' is an anagram of the word 'Classroom' and Astronomers is an anagram of 'Moon starers'.

Answer:

The number ten goes on the top line and should be placed after the 6. This is because each of the lines runs in numerical order, so the 10 logically goes at the end. But why should it go on the top row?

All the numbers in each row have, when written as a word, an equal number of letters: three letters on the top row, four on the second and five on the third. Ten has three letters and so must logically be placed on the top row.

𝓕𝓾𝓷 𝓯𝓪𝓬𝓽: fantastic or weird?

If you shuffle a pack of playing cards, there are so many possible combinations that you may well get a sequence that has never been seen before in the whole history of the world! (For the record, in round figures, the number of possible combinations is **8...followed by 67 zeros.** Simply unimaginable! But true.)

Two groups of words

Consider the following list of words:

BODY
AWE
DAY
FEAR
HAND
HOW
LONE
ONE
THING
TIRE
WHERE
WHOLE

The task is to divide the above list into two categories by adding a single new word to the beginning of each word listed, to make one group, or to the end, making a second group. The addition must make a new word.
The question is – what is the word needed to do this?

What goes up, but never comes down?

Answer:

The word you need to add is **some**. This gives you two groups of new words, one with the word added in front and one at the end of the word:

1. **AWESOME, FEARSOME, HANDSOME, LONESOME, TIRESOME and WHOLESOME**

2. **SOMEBODY, SOMEDAY, SOMEHOW, SOMEONE, SOMETHING and SOMEWHERE.**

What do you throw out when you want to use it but take in when you don't want to use it?

Answer

A ship's anchor

Moving glasses

Consider the row of five glasses shown here, some empty some containing water:

The task is to change the row so that it is changed to appear as below, and to do so by moving only *one* glass.

How can that be done? You can work this out on paper or find five glasses and try it for real.

What belongs to you but is mostly used by other people?

Answer:

Take the glass on the far left, pour the water into empty glass situated four places along from the left and move the now empty glass into fifth position on the far right. The solution needs not just moving but pouring too.

𝓕𝓾𝓷 𝓯𝓪𝓬𝓽: fantastic or weird?

The famous Paris landmark the Eiffel Tower took 22 months to build, and the framework is made from 7300 tons of iron.

The huge structure (it is 1083 feet high including antennas) becomes up to six inches taller on a hot summer's day as the structure expands in the heat.

Odd word out.

Next is another word problem.

Which is the odd one out amongst those listed words: **stun, ton, evil, letter, mood, bad, snap, and straw?**

Answer:

It is the word <u>letter</u>. All the other words in the list form a word when read backwards.

How can you make 1000 using eight number 8s?

With the sum 8 + 8 + 8 + 88 + 888

𝓕𝓾𝓷 𝓯𝓪𝓬𝓽: fantastic or weird?

The human eye is so sensitive it can see the flame of a candle in the dark thirty miles away. Except that you cannot do this as, in flat terrain, the horizon is only 4 to 5 miles away for a person of average height; the candle would be over the horizon.

Time for some more numbers?

Check out the following equation. It looks odd to begin with but by adding one – and only one – short straight line it can be made to make logical sense. Can you work out how to do so?

The formula: **9.50 = 10 10 10**

What can you keep having given it away?

Answer

Answer:

There is a clue in the title. Add the line to the middle ten and it all makes sense.

9.50 = 10 T0 10

Just in time.

What is it that completely disappears if you say the word that describes it out loud?

Just straight lines

Below is a short row of six straight vertical lines, they can be any length·

There is no meaningful pattern to them - but there can be.

The task is to rearrange them to make *four* triangles.

Fun fact: fantastic or weird?

If you counted all the way to one million, taking only a second for each number counted, it would take you more than 11 years (and a billion would take over *31 years)*. And perhaps we should add some time for a few bathroom breaks to that!

Answer:

There are still six lines, but now they are arranged to answer the question. See below.

But there is another way to do this. Turn over for the answer.

Answer (four triangles)

You could also arrange them like this:

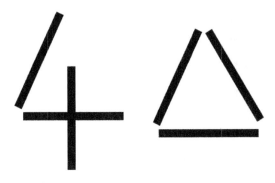

Happy Birthday

Imagine: how can a person have been 13 years old on their last birthday and yet they will be 15 years old on their next birthday?

Spelled out forwards it is something you do every day, spelt backwards it is something you hate. What is it?

Answer:

The person is in no way peculiar – it is just that it must be their 14th birthday *today*. Incidentally, though you may feel your birthday is special – if there are 23 people in a room, there is a 50% chance of two of them having the same birthday and for a 99.9% chance you only need 70 people.

Fun fact: fantastic or weird?

A 'tittle' is the name of the dot above the letters i and j. Who even knew they had a name?

Found in the attic

Imagine that you are rummaging in the attic, and you find five short chains each with four links. They appear to be gold and you think that, if you joined them together, they would make a nice necklace.

You take them to a jeweller who confirms they are real gold and tells you it will cost ten pounds for each link they break and then use to rejoin the whole into one long chain.

How should this be done to get the lowest price? And what is the cost?

𝓕𝓾𝓷 𝓯𝓪𝓬𝓽: fantastic or weird?

The human body has 206 bones, but a new-born baby has 300 (some fusing together as they grow).

Answer:

It is best to work with one chain first, breaking all four of its links will give one link oooh to join the four remaining sections together - so the cost is just £40.00.

Fun fact: fantastic or weird?

'Eleven plus two' is an anagram of 'twelve plus one', and both add up to 13, which seems only appropriate as both phrases contain 13 letters.

Just one letter

Consider the following sequence of letters:

A B C D _

How do you add one more to the correct alphabetic sequence, but *without using the letter E.*

I am seven letter word. I am very heavy. Take away two letters from me and you will get 8. Take away one letter and you will get 80. What am I?

Answer:

You just write the letter F. Putting it on top of the line creates the letter E.

𝓕𝓾𝓷 𝓯𝓪𝓬𝓽: fantastic or weird?

A historic language oddity: The word a 'hundred' comes from an old Norse word 'hundrath' – but that meant 120!

Counting and writing

When one of the author's granddaughters was very young, she counted to 100 by saying: *One, two … skip a few… ninety-nine, a hundred!* But I am sure you can count well.

The task: is to consider all the numbers from 1 to 99 as words and arrange them into alphabetical order – which number remains in its original place?

What is it that you can strike up, but not strike down?

A conversation

Answer:

The number which remains in its numerical sequence is 69 – sixty-nine. Promise. You will have quite a lot of writing to do if you want to check! Or did you do that already?

𝓕𝓾𝓷 𝓯𝓪𝓬𝓽: fantastic or weird?

Humans cannot walk in a straight line without looking. Given enough space you always tend to walk in a circle. You could try it yourself wearing a blindfold next time you are in the park (but definitely with someone to watch that you do not walk into anything).

Empty the glass

Arrange four matchsticks in the shape below (to roproont a ctommod glass)

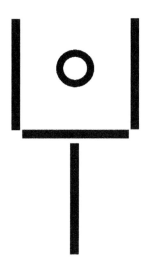

Put a coin as it were into the glass, then the task is to move no more than *two* matchsticks to get the coin outside the glass shape – and, no, you *cannot touch or move the coin.*

Fun fact: fantastic or weird?

The number four contains four letters and is the only number that has this matching of letters and its meaning as a number.

Answer:

The diagram below shows how to do it (moving the match that forms the base of the "glass" to the right and moving the match forming the lefthand side of the "glass" to create the image upside down).

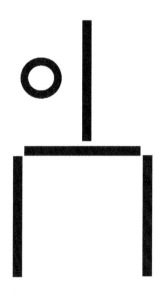

A sundial has the fewest moving parts of any timepiece. Which has the most?

An hourglass, with thousands of grains of sand.

Work out the word

The task here is to work out which single word has the first two letter indicating a male person, the first three letters indicating a female person, the first four letters meaning a great person and the whole word meaning a great female person. What is the word?

What runs round a garden but never never moves?

Answer:

The word is Heroine.

Fun fact: fantastic or weird?

The continent of Australia is wider than the moon (though it is easier to get to!).
The moon is 2159 miles wide and Australia is almost exactly 2500 miles across.

A talking game

If you can talk, then you can do this. What's that? All you need to do is just talk without stopping and do so in a way that makes proper sense for one minute... but you must do so without using any word which contains the letter **A.** It is surely easy. Whoops, easy has a letter **a** in it so that's no good and you can't say:

- Let me tell you **a**bout ...
- I'm going to t**a**lk ...
- This is **a**ll right ...
- Or use the words **a**nyway, **a**lways or complic**a**ted.

It's a bit tricky, though there is something you can do to make it easy - but you <u>can</u> do it. You could set a time limit for this (maybe five minutes?) in which case you will need something to count down the time, a watch with a second hand or a mobile phone perhaps, though you could ponder it all day if you need and want to do so. It can be fun to do this with other people either as a race or taking turns – who will be first to make it work? Here's a hint: remember there is a trick which, if you discover that, you can count on to enable you to do it easily; there is a clue here! Can you work out what that is?

What do an island and the letter T have in common?

What has to be broken before you can use it?

Answer:

Did you manage it? Who did best? *It is tricky, isn't it?* But there is a way to make it easy... all you need to do is to count, just say:

One, two, three, four, five, six, seven, eight, nine, ten, eleven, twelve ... and so on.

All you need to do is continue counting until the minute is up, there will not be a letter **A** until maybe you say, "**a** hundred", so there is plenty of counting to fill a minute. If you just say 'hundred' or 'one hundred', rather than 'a hundred', then you need to count a lot more to get to an a – the first comes in the word 'thousand'.

So, the trick makes it easy. Well done if you worked it out.

What number is next?

Here is a sequence of numbers.

181

920

212

223

____

There is a logical reason for the order in which the numbers are arranged. And the next one must follow the pattern. Can you see what that pattern is and work out which three-digit number should logically be put next?

Fun fact: fantastic or weird?

A googleplex is the number one followed by 100 zeros. If you tried to write all the numbers out, number by number, you would need a book that weighed more than the earth!

Fun fact: fantastic or weird?

On a dice the numbers on opposite sides always add up to the number 7.

Answer:

Look at the numbers again:

181

920

212

223

The solution becomes obvious if you read the numbers in pairs, two at a time, through the sequence.

Then they read: 18, 19, 20, 21, 22, 23 so the next the number must logically be **<u>242</u>** (that is 24 and the first number of 25). And so on.

This is a good one to try out on friends; all you need is a piece of paper and a pencil.

A very orderly number

Which number when it is spelt out as a word has all its letters in alphabetical order? As a little clue: don't doze off as you think about this!

Answer:

The correct answer is the number 40 – FORTY (as in "forty winks").

Every which way

What do these five words have in common?

Here is a clue: if you do one particular thing to them the result is common in every case. But what?

- **Assess**
- **Banana**
- **Dresser**
- **Grammar**
- **Potato**

Fun fact: fantastic or weird?

The number 13 is supposed to be unlucky; the fear of 13 is called triskaidekaphobia.

Answer

With all the words if you take the first letter and place it at the end of the word you create the same word when read backwards, as in **Assess - ssessA.**

What breaks and never falls, and what falls and never breaks?

Day breaks and night falls

A sense of direction

The problem here is to answer one simple question. There are some details first which you need to read carefully.

Okay, let's begin - imagine you are the captain of a ship, your ship is sailing due north in the middle of the Atlantic Ocean at a speed of 12 knots. After steaming in that direction for 30 minutes, the captain gives the order to the engine room to alter course through 180 degrees and then maintain the same speed for one hour.

After that hour has passed the captain issues new orders, another change of course through 180 degrees returning to the ship's original course "in order to avoid a coming storm"

Now the question: **How old is the ship's captain?**

What runs, but
never walks.
Murmurs, but never
talks. Has a bed,
but never sleeps.
And has a mouth,
but never eats?

Answer

A River

Answer:

If you feel you can't possibly know the answer, then read the instructions again. The firot words were "Imagine you are the captain of a ship", so the answer must be your own age.

If you did not get this right then don't feel too bad, commonly we all tend to pay less attention to the very first words of any message.

Moral: it is useful to know this. Listen (or read) carefully to *every bit of an important message* and you will miss less. Similarly think carefully about how you arrange your messages to others and maybe do not put the most important point in the first few words.

Fun fact: fantastic or weird?

Sharks are scary creatures, but they only kill five or six people a year on average, whereas more than 200 hundred people in the world are killed every year by falling coconuts! So, maybe one should be more careful on the beach than in the sea!

Metro access

There had to be at least one anagram in a book such as this, so here it is – or rather here they are as there are several. A clue is in the title. Can you work them out?

1. **Red admiral**
2. **Uncouth president**
3. **Real bacon**
4. **Synthetic cream**
5. **Grilled rhombus**
6. **Let alpacas cry.**

As usual the answer is over the page.

What kind of coat is always wet when you put it on?

A coat of paint

Answer:

First the clue: the words **Metro Access** make an anagram of the words 'Soccer teams', and tho five answers are:

1. Real Madrid
2. Scunthorpe United
3. Barcelona
4. Manchester City
5. Middlesbrough
6. Crystal Palace

Describing shapes

This exercise involves some simple description. Look at the pattern of shapes that appears below and then - *without* showing it to them - describe it to someone else just in words and ask them to draw how they think it appears. See how quickly and how accurately they can draw something that looks identical.

If you describe it to more than one person, then you can make it a competition and see who gets the most accurate representation with their version looking most like the original.

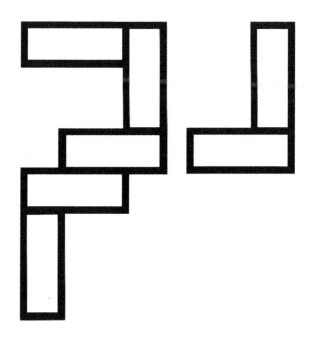

Answer:

This can be difficult unless the description given is accurate, and to achieve this you need to give *exactly* how you describe things some thought. It will be easier if you note that:

- All the shapes are the same (like bricks)
- All are the same size
- They only appear in three different positions.

The moral here is that often it is worth thinking about *how* you say something before you say it. Remember the old saying: Engage your brain before you open your mouth!

Postscript: just one more...

The next and final problem is a little different in that you need to obtain some (simple) equipment to make it work. So, you will need to know how it works and can then try it out on friends and family. But... if you want to try it out yourself first then do NOT turn over and look at the next page – get someone to set everything up for you and pose the question.

The jigsaw puzzle challenge:

a race against time and maybe friends

For this challenge you will need two jigsaw puzzles. They should have pictures that are similar in subject and style (perhaps both depicting Disney characters such as Micky Mouse and Donald Duck).

Size: 100 pieces is ideal (if they are too large then the whole puzzle will become too time consuming).

Once you have chosen the puzzles then you should:

Completely assemble one of the puzzles. Do this on a board of some sort (like a stiff piece of cardboard just a little larger than the completed puzzle).

Then turn the puzzle upside down (if you put something rigid like another piece of card on top you can do this and keep the puzzle intact)

Now write numbers on the pieces, in order along the rows starting at the top left:

1 2 3 4 5 6 7 8 9 10 11 12 13 14 15 16 17 18 19 20 21 22 and so on.

Next, dismantle the jigsaw, mix the pieces and put them all in one of the boxes, choosing the box for the puzzle where the picture on the box matches the puzzle which remains untouched and without added numbers - *together with* the pieces for the second puzzle. Mix the pieces up all together.

You now have all the pieces for both puzzles muddled together in one box. The second box (which depicts the picture of the puzzle you have numbered) should be kept separate.

Now you need to describe the task to whoever will do it. This can be one other person, a small group who will work together (5 or six is enough) or perhaps two small teams who will compete to win.

Note: *if you do this with two, or more teams, then you will need two jigsaws per team.*

The task

Show people both box lids - briefly - explaining that they will only have one available during the task.

Tell people that the job is twofold:

- *to complete the both the jigsaws in the shortest possible time and...*
- *to work out why some pieces have a number on the reverse side.*

You should set a time limit (or the whole thing might go on too long) of, say 20 minutes. **Note:** this time matches the 100-piece jigsaws it is suggested using; if very young people are involved then smaller jigsaws should be used. After that, if neither team has completed the task more time could be allowed or the nearest to a solution is the winner. Whoever has the best result at the end of the 20 minutes wins!

Okay? *One, two, three... go!*

Note: *Clearly once the reason why one jigsaw has numbers is worked out then that jigsaw can be completed (upside down) in moments, with the picture available for the second puzzle then a one-hundred-piece jigsaw should not take too long to complete.*

If a group is involved, then some organisation helps, one person can do the numbered puzzle and the better organised a group of people are the faster they will complete the one for which the picture is available; for example, one person might search for and complete all the, straight-sided, edge pieces. Remember the old saying: too many cooks spoil the broth.

Afterword

Well, we are at the end. We hope all this has exercised your brain a bit. Like your body, brains are made of about 78% water so if you got some – most? - of these problems correct then your water content is working well!

The Authors

Patrick Forsyth is the author of both fiction and non-fiction books across several genres and here worked with **Trevor Peters,** who was a teacher for many years and added valuable practical experience of using the sort of puzzle included here to the job of assembling and writing this book. Both writers involved their children and grandchildren in the project.

Acknowledgements

This all started with grandchildren: Fabian and Tilly (PF) and Harry and Danny (TP). It was Tilly who started it, by using the phrase "It's a bit tricky" so much whenever she tackled something new when she was about four or five years old. So, while various others helped in a number of ways, not least by being guinea pigs and trying out many of the puzzles here before we decided to include them, let's just say a big thank you to Fabian and Tilly and Harry and Danny – you are all such an important part of our lives.

Patrick Forsyth and **Trevor Peters**

Printed in Great Britain
by Amazon